CRUISE EXCURSIONS ON YOUR OWN

European Cruise

Nancy T. Berg

DEDICATION

This book is dedicated to the loving people in my life who have inspired me to see the world and to share my experiences with others.

A HANDBOOK FOR
CRUISE EXCURSIONS ON YOUR OWN

TABLE OF CONTENTS

Typical Western Mediterranean Sailing Itinerary

Day	Port ***	Arrive	Depart	
1	Barcelona, Spain		7:00 PM	
2	Cruising			
3	Naples, Capri, Italy	7:00 AM	7:00 PM	Docked
4	Civitavecchia (Rome), Italy	7:00 AM	7:00 PM	Docked
5	Livorno (Florence/Pisa), Italy	7:00 AM	7:00 PM	Docked
6	Villefranche (Nice), France	7:00 AM	7:00 PM	Tendered
7	Provence (Toulon), France	7:00 AM	5:00 PM	Docked
8	Barcelona, Spain	6:00 AM		

MEDITERRANEAN CRUISE PORTS OF

BARCELONA, SPAIN & NAPLES, ROME, & FLORENCE, ITALY

So you found the perfect cruise at the perfect price to a beautiful location you've never been to before. And now that you are ready to fly to your departure port and get onboard your ship, you realize that you are going to destinations you have never been before and know nothing about! What next? You decide that you will sign up for the excursions offered by the cruise ship and see the world! But, when you check out the available cruise ship excursions online, you realize that you will have to spend between $50.00 and $350.00 per person for a single excursion in each port – prices vary by the number of destinations, the mode of transportation and the number of people they group for the tour. Suddenly, that perfect cruise at the perfect price is looking very expensive. If you want to keep the expense of your cruise down, you can either settle for doing fewer excursions and seeing less of the sights each port has to offer, or you can use this guide book to see the world for next to nothing!

First and foremost, the point of this travel guide is to save you a lot of money when you embark on your next cruise! You don't want to spend hundreds of extra dollars once you board the cruise ship – especially since you spent a lot of time search for that reasonably priced cruise to your destination. So, use this guide to enjoy your cruise without paying ridiculous prices for cruise ship excursions which can add hundreds of dollars to your vacation.

This travel guide will provide you with detailed step-by-step instructions on how to make the most of your eight to ten hours in each port you will be visiting on your chosen cruise. The guide is meant to (1) save you money; and (2) to help you see all of the amazing sights that a port city has to offer. Take this handbook with you as you embark on your cruise of the Mediterranean. Since the itinerary varies, this book will concentrate on the ports that are included in most Western Mediterranean Cruises – Barcelona, Naples, Rome, and Florence.

This handbook obviously is not for everyone. Some people find it much easier to pay the money to enjoy the convenience of a tour planned by the ship -- the bus will be at the ship to meet you and take you directly to your destination. But, this convenience will come at a very high cost, especially if you are paying for more than one person. At the beginning of each chapter, I show the per person price and time allotted for a typical cruise excursion. The information in chapter then details how you can do the same excursion on your own for a fraction of the cost. Therefore, if you are somewhat adventuresome and enjoy a little challenge, you can see a lot more for a lot less money using this handbook as your guide.

My other travel guides concentrate on ports typically included in Mediterranean cruises, including France, Italy, Croatia, and Slovenia; and additional guides are available for other European destinations, as well as Eastern and Western Caribbean cruises.

THE ARGUMENT FOR DOING IT ON YOUR OWN

For your convenience, I have gathered information from hundreds of websites and other sources to compile the details that are contained on the pages in this travel guide.

This guide provides you with important travel tips for each port that will help you make the most of your time in each port and still have time to relax onboard and enjoy the drink of the day and all of the delightful meals the ship has to offer.

One of the first things you'll discover when planning to get the most out of your cruise is that cruise ships are in business to make money -- and one of the biggest money-making items offered by the cruise lines, besides the drink of the day, are the excursions at each port. Whether you book a shore excursion on the ship or explore your port of call independently depends on you, your interests, and your comfort level in unfamiliar surroundings. If you decide to participate in the excursions offered by the cruise lines, you should be prepared to spend hundreds of extra dollars on your cruise to participate in these excursions. Prices for each excursion can range in price from $25.00 to $250.00 **per person**. So, depending on the size of your travel group, taking a tour sponsored by your cruise line in every port can quickly inflate the cost of your cruise.

As important as saving money is being able to see all of the sights that each port has to offer. And, because of the way that the ships schedule their excursions at each port and the amount of time spent on one excursion, if you choose to participate in a cruise line excursion, you will be limited to one excursion per port and you are going to miss out on seeing a lot of the sights and culture that each city has to offer.

European tours focus on sightseeing unlike Caribbean tours which have excursion options like snorkeling with sting rays, jet ski rentals, or transportation to private beaches. In Europe, excursions offered by the cruise line offer full-day tours visiting the museums and cathedrals with a lot of time allotted for gathering busloads of tourists, and dutifully following flag-waving guides at a snail's pace around the sights, as they stop to wait for that one participant who holds everyone else up because he or she gets

4

lost from the group or because he or she wanted to read every sign on every building and statue.

Why do I say that if the cruise lines are the experts on the subject of cruising? Because a cruise ship excursion has to plan a lot of additional time for gathering the participants for the transportation to the sight; gathering all of the participants to move from one sight to the next; providing the group with ample free time in the area you have just spent hours walking around in so that you can spend money on shopping and eating; and finally gathering everyone for the transportation back to the ship. By the time you return to the ship, all of the other excursions will have departed the ship, and you will have spent an entire day touring one sight in a city that has so much more to offer.

Therefore, the point of this book is to avoid the above scenario and to help you see it all at a fraction of the cost and still have time to get back to the ship and enjoy a swim in the pool with the drink of the day in hand! This book is for the traveler who has embarked on a cruise because they want to see everything at each port city in the countries they are visiting. If you plan ahead using this book as your guide, you can actually see all of the sights for the cost of a bus or train ticket from the port to the various sights.

In this book, I have included step-by-step plans for exploring the sights on a typical cruise of the Mediterranean Sea – one that sets sail from Barcelona, Spain and visits the ports of Naples, Capri, Italy, Civitavecchia (Rome), Italy, and Livorno (Florence/Pisa), Italy.

Where Do You Start?

There is so much to see in each of the ports that you may wonder how you could possibly navigate an unfamiliar city on your own, but if you follow the detailed plans included in this book for each port, you will enjoy seeing all of the interesting sights instead of one sight at each port.

One of the first questions you'll ask yourself when you're planning a cruise vacation is, "Where do I want to go and what do I want to see when I get there?" To help you make the decision of when and where to go on your cruise, there are numerous travel websites and cruiseline websites that have compiled cruises available for various destinations, as well as the prices you will pay for your cruise on a particular date and in your choice of a stateroom. The prices are unbelievably reasonable for a floating hotel with meals included. But, unless you are the type of cruiser who is satisfied with eating the continuous offering of meals and relaxing around the pool onboard your cruise ship, then the price of the cruise is actually the only thing cheap about cruising.

Because, if you plan to indulge in drinking the cocktails of the day, purchasing the pictures taken of you at every photo op, gambling, and taking excursions to see Europe, the cost of the cruise just tripled.

One way to cut back on the additional costs of your cruise is to use this guide for planning your own excursions at each port.

TIP #1:

While in Europe, remember that the cheapest way to get local money is by using your ATM debit card. The banks will process it immediately at a good rate. However, you will still be paying an ATM transaction fee, and some banks may charge an extra fee for an international transaction. An example of currency at the ATM using a Debit Card would be **Converter: $1.00 = .73924 Therefore, $100 = $73.9240.** *To find out what your home currency is worth in Euros, or any other currency, check online before you go.*

BARCELONA, SPAIN

Typical Cruise Ship Excursion:

Full-Day Barcelona Audio Guide Walking Tour:
Transportation to various districts and then with a
detailed map, take an easy walking tour of the
ancient cobble-stoned streets and historic sights of
Barcelona's famous districts. There are more than
30 points of interest, including the city's most
famous promenade, Las Ramblas, to the beauty
and majesty of Barcelona's Cathedral and its
cloisters. **Duration: 10 hours Prices starting**
from: $120.00 USD (Adult)

For a fraction of the cost of the above cruise line excursion, you can see all of the same sights, either on foot [and metro] or on an open-air bus.

First, though, if your cruise departs from Barcelona, you need to get from the airport to the cruise ship port. Here's how:

Travel To & From The Barcelona Airport

If Barcelona, Spain, is your departure port, you will fly into **Barcelona-El Prat Airport** and you will need to get to your cruise ship docked at the **Adossat Quay Terminal**. You will have to decide before leaving home whether you want to purchase ground transportation from the cruise line; or if you want to make your own arrangements. The website for your cruise line will advise you of which terminal [A, B, C or D] cruise ship is docked at the Adossat Quay Terminal. Here are your choices for transportation:

1. Getting to the Cruise Ship Port if you purchase "Cruise Line Ground Transportation" – If you made your flight arrangements through the cruise line, you will also likely purchase the ground transportation. In this case, the cruise line staff will meet you with signs in the Baggage Claim Area or outside of Customs to direct you to your transportation between the airport and the ship.

2. If you have made your own flight arrangements and want to make your own ground transportation plans, the best option for traveling to and from the Barcelona Airport to the port is by taxi. The journey will take you about 25 minutes and will cost you (**no matter how many people are in your party**) around 25 - 30 Euros = approximately **$40.00 total** [depending upon the exchange rate], with a bag supplement of approximately 0.90 Euros per bag = $1.00.

Upon arrival at your designated ship, there will be cruise line staff waiting outside to collect your luggage and you can take the time to check in now, which will take longer because of the many guests who will be arriving at the same time; or you can check in after sightseeing. You can check in to your cruise up to ninety minutes before departure.

Most cruise ships depart Barcelona at around 5:00 to 7:00 p.m. and you can check in to your cruise up to ninety minutes before departure. Therefore, if you arrive at the airport in Barcelona, Spain by noon, you will have four to five hours of free time before your sail time. Therefore, if you plan ahead, you will be able to see most of the sights of Barcelona before you board your ship.

Following are your plans for a safe and efficient sightseeing tour of Barcelona, Spain before your ship sails out of this port.

SIGHTSEEING IN BARCELONA

The Map of Barcelona below shows the ten districts that make up the city. Each district is further divided into smaller neighborhoods called *Barri.* The oldest part of Barcelona, **including the cruise ship port**, is found in the **Ciutat Vella** district, while the Eixample district is home to upscale homes, shops and numerous examples of the architecture of Antoni Gaudi, Barcelona's favorite son. The main **train station, *Estacion de Sants,*** is located in the Sants Montjuic district, and the Barcelona Airport is located to the West of Sants Montjuic.

More detailed descriptions of each district appear in the Walking Tours section below, but first consider the Hop-on Hop-Off Tour Bus Tour.

Barcelona City Hop-on Hop-off Tour

NOTE: A typical cruise line tour in an <u>enclosed</u> bus will cost you approximately U.S. $50.00 <u>per person</u> and <u>does not include any stops </u>or interior visits to any of the monuments or museums.

By far, the best way to see all of the sights in Barcelona is aboard a **Hop-on Hop-Off Tour Bus**. I highly recommend the bus tour because you can hop off at any stop and spend as much or as little time at places of interest before jumping aboard for the next stop - the choice is yours! You will ride in an open-top double-decker bus with over 44 stops on one of 3 different tour routes.

Getting to Plaça de Catalunya To Board Hop-On Hop-Off Bus

Take the **shuttle bus (Blue Bus) at the cruise terminal** to Plaza de Colon [which has the Christopher Columbus Monument] and then walk the short distance along La Rambla Street until arriving at Plaça de Catalunya, the busiest square surrounded by monumental buildings [you will see tour buses lined up]. The Blue Bus runs regularly all day from all the cruise port terminals and back. Or you can travel by **taxi** – the fare for a taxi from the port to the city centre is around €8.00. Or, you could **walk** 1.24 miles to the city centre but that is recommended only if you are in good physical condition because it is a long walk.

A **One-Day Ticket** for Unlimited use on Barcelona City Hop-on Hop-off Tour for an Adult [Age 13 and up] is approximately $30.00 and for a child is $20.00 [Free for ages 0-3]. Credit cards are accepted.

3 Bus Tour Routes to Choose From

The three tour routes are inter-connected so you can hop to another route easily between each of the stops! Departures are approximately every 25 minutes.

Northern Route (Red Line) Tour is 2 hours long and includes:

- **Placa de Catalunya** - a large plaza surrounded by monumental buildings, is Barcelona's busiest square. It is located between the old city (Ciutat Vella) and the 19th century Eixample district.
- **Casa Batllo** - Many of architect, Gaudí's masterpiece buildings are located in Eixample. One of the most remarkable is the magnificent Casa Batlló; and Fundacio Antoni Tapies - a building with a richly decorated crown
- **Passeig de Gracia** - La Pedrera - This was the last private building designed by Gaudí, from then on he would only work on the Sagrada Familia.
- **Sagrada Familia** - Antoni Gaudí's unfinished masterpiece, is one of Barcelona's most popular tourist attractions. Construction on this church will continue for at least another decade, but it has already become Barcelona's most important landmark.
- **Gracia** - Make sure you take a trip down the avenue known as Passeig de Gràcia, one of the most architecturally important streets in the city.
- **Parc Guell** - is one of the world's most intriguing parks. The park's colorful main staircase and the fanciful pavilions that were designed by Antoni Gaudí look like they belong in some fairy tale.
- **Tramvia Blau – Tibidabo** - Tibidabo is a mountain just northwest of Barcelona, crowned with the Church of the Sacred Heart. But the mountain's main draw is the Parc d'Attractions, a more than 100 year old funfair; a historic tram - the Tramvia Blau (Blue Tram) - runs up the hill to the Plaça Doctor Andreu, the starting point of the Funicular railway that takes you to the top of the Tibidabo.
- **Sarria** - Barcelona's Sarria-Sant Gervasi neighborhood
- **Monestir de Pedralbes** - Col.leccio Thyssen - is a former monastery built in the early 14th century. Today the complex is open to the public and it sheds a light on what monastic life must have been like during the Middle Ages.
- **Palau Reial - Pavellons Guell** - The Güell Pavilions were built between 1884 and 1887 by Antoni Gaudí, best known as the architect of the Sagrada Familia. The pavilions were built for a summer residence of the wealthy Catalan industrialist Eusebi Güell.

- Barcelona Football Club
- Francesc Macia – Diagonal - A large number of sculptures are planted around the central paved area, seemingly at random. The most prominent of these is the Monument a Francesc Macià, honoring the former president of the Generalitat (the Catalan government). The sculpture was created in 1991 by Josep Subirachs, the architect in charge of the construction of the Sagrada Família.
- MACBA – CCCB – Museum of Contemporary Art.

The Southern Route (Blue Line) Tour is 2 hours long and includes:

- Placa de Catalunya - a large plaza surrounded by monumental buildings, is Barcelona's busiest square. It is located between the old city (Ciutat Vella) and the 19th century Eixample district.
- Casa Batllo - Fundacio Antoni Tapies - a building restored by Antoni Gaudí and Josep Maria Jujol, built in 1877 and remodelled in the years 1904–1906
- Passeig de Gracia - La Pedrera - most important shopping and business area regarded as the most expensive street in Barcelona and in Spain
- Francesc Macia – Diagonal – a square; contains a pond modelled after the shape of Minorca, the birthplace of its architect, Nicolau Rubió i Tudurí, as well as femenine sculpture called *Joventut* ("youth") designed by Josep Manuel Benedicto, added in 1953
- Estacio de Sants - is the main railway station; hub of travel
- Creu Coberta - the main artery in the Sants district, and one of the city's most popular shopping areas
- Placa d'Espanya - For centuries the site was used for public hangings until the gallows were moved; now it is is a busy square located at the foot of the Montjuïc Hill.
- Caixa Forum - Pavello Van Der Rohe - also known as the Barcelona Pavilion, is an iconic landmark of the Modern Movement and has been a source of inspiration to generations of architects; Mies van der Rohe is considered the father of Modern architecture
- Poble Espanyol - "Spanish Town" is an open-air architectural museum, located on the mountain of Montjuïc
- MNAC - Museu Nacional d'Art de Catalunya

- <u>Anella Olimpica</u> - is an Olympic Park located in the hill of Montjuïc, Barcelona, that was the main site for the 1992 Summer Olympics
- <u>Funicular de Montjuïc</u> - is a funicular railway
- <u>Fundacio Joan Miro</u> - museum of modern art honoring Joan Miró
- <u>Miramar</u> - Jardins Costa i Llobera
- <u>World Trade Center</u> - building structure was inspired by the shape of a boat surrounded by the Mediterranean Sea, and created by renowned architect Henry N. Cobb who emphasized aesthetics
- <u>Colom - Museu Maritim</u> – ship museum; the construction of the shipyards was Barcelona's naval supremacy throughout the Mediterranean expansion.
- <u>Port Vell</u> - is a waterfront harbour
- <u>Museu d'Historia de Catalunya</u> – history museum
- <u>Port Olimpic</u> - is a marina located east of the Port of Barcelona; it hosted the sailing events for the 1992 Summer Olympics; The Peix (fish) sculpture sits in the port and was built in 1992 at Barcelona's waterfront. The large steel structure is indicative of the themes of many other Frank O. Gehry works.
- <u>Place de la Citadel</u> - is Barcelona's most central park. The park includes a zoo, a lake, a large fountain and several museums. The Catalan Parliament is seated in a building at the center of the park.
- <u>Pla de Palau</u> - was long ago the main square of trading Barcelona, as it provided the only access from the sea to the city for people or merchandise through the Sea Gate
- <u>Barri Gotic</u> - area is also known as the Gothic Quarter and is the area in which the old town of Barcelona is situated; Picasso lived and worked in Barri Gotic from 1895 to 1904 and Joan Miró was born and lived here during his youth.

The Forum Route (Green Line) Tour is 40 minutes long and includes:

- <u>Port Olimpic</u> - is a marina located east of the Port of Barcelona; it hosted the sailing events for the 1992 Summer Olympics
- <u>Platja del Bogatell</u> - Barcelona's beach hosted volleyball for 1992 Summer Olympics beach

- <u>Forum</u> – open public space and public building
- <u>Parc Diagonal Mar</u> - epitomises the new Barcelona and is quite unlike any other city park.
- <u>Poblenou</u> - is a neighborhood that borders the Mediterranean sea; many artists and young professionals have converted the former factories and warehouses into lofts, galleries, and shops.

WALKING TOURS OF BARCELONA

You could spend about $100.00 per person for a guided walking tour of Barcelona's main sights in several of the districts, but save your money and follow the following easy guidelines and maps in this chapter to see the parts of the city that interest you. Take the **shuttle bus** (Blue Bus) at the cruise terminal to Plaza de Colon [Christopher Columbus Monument] and then walk up La Rambla Street to the 3 **Metro stops** described below. Spend a full day sightseeing by **traveling the Metro** to the stops around the city:

METRO STOPS

Drassanes **Metro** stop (**Green Line L3**) - At the Southern most end of La Rambla, near to Christopher Columbus Memorial.

Liceu **Metro** stop (**Green Line L3**) - Midway along Las Ramblas, just outside the Liceu Theatre.

Catalunya **Metro** on both the (**Green Line, L3**) and (**Red Line, L1**). At the northern most tip of Las Ramblas. **Catalunya is also the point at which you can catch the Hop on Hop Off Tourist Bus** [should you decide you have had enough walking!]

Map of Metro System on Next Page

14

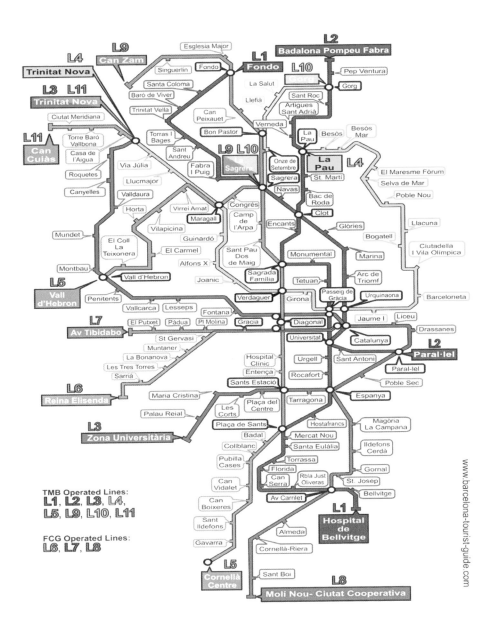

TMB Operated Lines:
L1, **L2**, **L3**, **L4**,
L5, **L9**, **L10**, **L11**

FCG Operated Lines:
L6, **L7**, **L8**

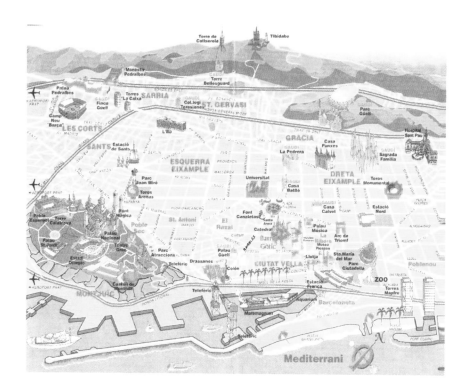

When you get off at a metro stop, use the descriptions below of each District for sights you can see in each.

WALKING TOURS

1. CIUTAT VELLA - The name means "Old City and the **Barri Gotic,** or **Gothic Quarter**, is located in Ciutat Vella. Barcelona's Gothic Quarter is filled with medieval buildings, squares, and the area around the Catedral de la Seu has Roman ruins and the Gothic structures of the late Middle Ages that marked the peak of Barcelona's power in the 15th century. **Places of Interest for a Tour of the Gothic Quarter or Old City include:**

* See Descriptions of Each in Hop-On Hop-Off Section

- Muralles romanes
- Museu d'Història de la Ciutat
- Casa de la Pia Almoina
- Casa de l'Ardiaca
- Palau Episcopal
- Sant Felip Neri
- Sant Sever
- Claustre de la catedral
- Temple d'August
- Verger del Palau Reial Major
- Palau del Lloctinent
- Placa del Rei
- PalauReial Major
- Capella de Santa Agata
- Carrer Llibreteria
- Pl. Sant Jaume
- Antic Hospital de la Santa Creu - Biblioteca
- Museu Marítim
- Fossar de les Moreres – cemetery
- Museu Picasso
- Palau de la Música Catalana – Music Palace
- Palau Güell - Gaudí mansion built 1886-89
- Plaça Sant Jaume 2000 yrs ago, center of
- Santa Maria del Mar - example of Catalan Gothic architecture
- Barceloneta – one of Barcelona's liveliest beaches

Map of Gothic Quarter on Next Page

Gòtic

2. THE EIXAMPLE - BARCELONA MODERNISM AND GAUDI WALKING TOUR

Eixample (the Extension) is a fashionable residential area where many of the city's most expensive shops, hotels, restaurants and nightspots can be found. This area became the focus of "modernist" Barcelona at the end of the 19th century and now is Barcelona's most famous neighborhood. The uniform grid pattern of the streets, as well as the Art Nouveau (Modernista) architecture that can be found throughout the neighborhood are the hallmarks of this district.

Some of the best known works of the famous local architect, Antoni Gaudi, can be found along the principal boulevard, the Passeig de Gràcia, and farther to the East, his famous Church of the Sagrada Famila. **Some of the places you may visit during this Modernism Barcelona Walking Tour include:**

* See Descriptions of Each in Hop-On Hop-Off Section

- Cases Pons I Pascual
- Cases Antoni Rocamora
- Casa Pia Batlló, Casa Heribert Pons, Casa Jaume Moysi, Casa Sebastià Pratsjusà, Casa Climent Arola
- Editorial Montaner 5 Simon - Fundació Antoni Tàpies
- Casa Pere Milà i Camps "La Pedrera"
- Palau de la Música Catalana
- Mansan a de la Discordia: Casa Lleo Morera, Casa Amatller, Casa Batllo
- Casa Vídua Mafà
- Temple Expiatori de la Sagrada Família

Map of Eixample District on Next Page

Modernisme

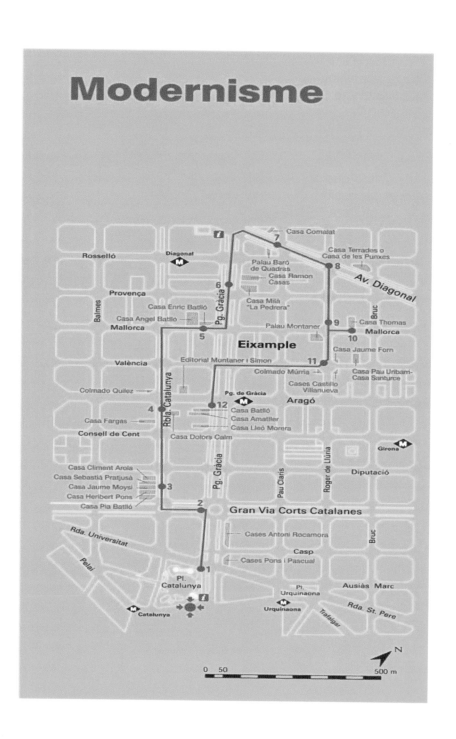

3. SANTS-MONTJUIC WALKING TOUR

Barcelona's largest collection of parks and gardens can be found in the hilltop neighborhood called Montjuic Mountain, along with most of the facilities used in the 1992 Olympic Games, five museums, the Poble Espanyol (a village showcasing different Spanish architectural styles) built for the 1929 International Exhibition, and the Castell de Montjuïc; a 17th century French fortress. The area is now a major destination for locals and tourists alike due to its numerous cafes, stores and clubs. The hilltop is accessible by bus, funicular, or cable car from Olympic Port and offers a panoramic view of the city and harbor. Montjuic is also home to the main international train station, Estacio Sants. **Some of the places you may visit during this Sants-Montjuic Barcelona Walking Tour include:**

* See Descriptions of Each in Hop-On Hop-Off Section

Museu Nacional d'Art de Catalunya
Fundació Miró – a gift from Joan Miró

4. LES CORTS - Primarily a residential district and the location of the University of Barcelona. Much of the area is very modern with large residential housing blocks.

5. SARRIA SANT GERVASI - A residential area whose narrow streets and picturesque houses give it the feel of a small village. The Collserola mountain area, with its views over the city, is popular for running, walking and biking.

6. GRACIA - An up and coming area located just to the North of Eixample. Gaudi's popular Parc Güell and the Plaça del Sol are located in this district. Elsewhere the district is home to traditional styled residential homes and unique shops and boutiques. The district's nightlife, is centered around Carrer Verdi, where trendy bars and restaurants popular among students and the Bohemian set attract revelers from all over Barcelona.

7. HORTA GUINARDO - An outlying district that was developed in the 1950s, it is notable for its high rise apartment buildings. The area has good public transportation links to central Barcelona, via subway or bus.

8. NOU BARRIS - An outlying residential area with a large working class immigrant population. Access to the center of Barcelona is good via bus or subway.

9. SANT ANDREU - Large outlying, primarily residential area.

10. SANT MARTI - This large district is bordered by the Mediterranean sea on the South, and Ciutat Vella on the West is newly chic and is home to the quiet, cosy Poble Sec neighborhood with its narrow 18th century streets and quiet neighborhood restaurants and dives, as well as the trendy and desirable El Poblenou neighborhood.

PICASSO AND PICASSO MUSEUM

See the places the famous artist frequented in Barcelona during your walking tour, before a visit to Barcelona's most visited museum - the Picasso Museum. The Picasso Walking Tour shows you the Bohemian Barcelona in which Picasso lived. **Some of the places you may visit during this Barcelona Walking Tour include:**

* See Descriptions of Each in Hop-On Hop-Off Section

- Quatre Gats Cafe
- Frisos del Col legi d'Arquitectes
- Sala Parés
- Escudellers Blancs
- Carrer Avinyó
- Carrer de la Plata
- Porxos d'En Xifre
- Llotja de Mar
- La Ribera Quarter
- Museu Picasso

Map of Picasso Area on Next Page

Picasso

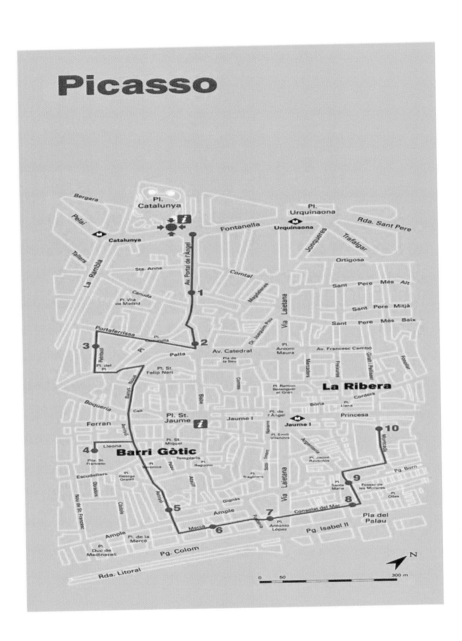

NAPLES/CAPRIS/SORRENTO, ITALY

Typical Cruise Ship Excursion:

*Island of Capri with Lunch - Walk to marina to board boat for <u>50-min cruise to Capri</u>. Explore Anacapri before return to Capri Town. Walk with guide thru streets & La Piazzetta Square. Have lunch in Capri Town. Explore Gardens of Augustus and fabled plaza, La Piazzetta before taking funicular down to Marina Grande to board boat for return to Naples. **Approximate Duration: 8 hours Prices starting from: $149.00 USD (Adult)***

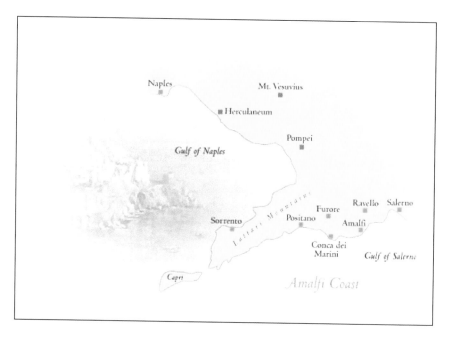

"The beauty of the Amalfi Coast region is best described by the myth from which the region gets its name: Hercules fell in love with a nymph named Amalfi, and when she died he is said to have buried her in the most beautiful place in the world."

Naples sits on the coast on the northern edge of the Bay of Naples and is the third most-populated city in Italy and the biggest city in Southern Italy – **why would you want to spend your**

24

entire time at this port on one excursion to the Island of Capri when there are so many other interesting sites, such as Mt. Vesuvius, Pompeii, the Amalfi Coast, and the quaint town of Sorrento, to visit while docked in Naples.

You could spend approximately $115 to $150 per person to visit each of the sights with a tour guide; or you could spend $350.00 per person to do the combination excursion of Pompeii, Amalfi Coast, Positano and Sorrento offered by the cruise ship. **But, I suggest you save your money and do it all on your own for the cost of a train ticket and ferry ticket**; and the entrance fee at Pompeii. At the entrance to Pompeii, there are free-lance local guides who will take you through the ruins and give you a guided tour for a fraction of the cost of a pre-purchased guided tour. Alternatively, you can follow the detailed tour provided in the brochure you can pick up at the entrance to Pompeii.

NAPLES EXCURSIONS ON YOUR OWN

The main cruise ship terminal is called Molo Beverello **and is conveniently located in the heart of downtown Naples**, so a short walk through the cruise terminal and port stations, through the narrow parking lot, and... Voila! You're now in downtown Naples, ready for a walking or bus tour of the sights in Naples and then a walk to the train station for your day trips away from Naples.

Downtown Naples Sights

Naples Transportation: Naples has good public transportation, including a large but crowded bus network, trams, a subway, funiculars (a cable railway on a steep incline), and a suburban train line, **the Ferrovia Circumvesuviana**. The train and bus stations are located in the huge Naples Central Station downstairs or at the Piazza Corso Garibaldi, on the eastern side of Naples. Trains will get you from Naples to Herculaneum, Pompeii, and Sorrento. Ferries and hydrofoils [high-speed boats] run from Naple's Molo Beverello [Naples Marina] to Capri Isle, Positano [beach] and to Sorrento.

WALKING OR BUS TOURS OF NAPLES

Naples City Hop-on Hop-off Tour

The **Naples City Hop-on Hop-off Tour** has three different tour routes to explore the city of Naples for a mere $27.00 USD per person. It is a great way to see the city and all of its amazing historical sights aboard an open-top double-decker bus that offers over 32 stops that you can hop on and hop off of all around the city as many times as you want. You can spend as much or as little time at places of interest before jumping aboard for the next stop. An informative printed guide about each of the stops is issued with the bus ticket, as well as a discount voucher booklet you can redeem at most of the main sights and landmarks around the city. The three tour routes are inter-connected so you can hop to another route easily between each of the stops!

Getting to Piazza Municipo from the cruise ship:

The Departure Point for the **Naples City Hop-on Hop-off Tour** is **Piazza Municipio** which is located at the Naples **Stazione Centrale** [train station] in the dingiest corner of the city. You can either take a **taxi** for a flat fee of approximately €10.50, or you can hop on **Tram #1** headed to your right (east), which will follow the port for a while before turning north (left) into the city, or you can just as easily **walk** the 1.5 miles to the Piazza Municipio.

The **3 Hop-on Hop-off Tours** offered in Naples are described below. All 3 routes are connected by Stop 1 [Piazza Municipo] and they take approximately 75 minutes to complete a full circuit – without hopping off at any of the sights. You can board the bus at any one of the stops around the city.

(1) **Line A - Art Tour** (11 stops) - Runs from 9:45 a.m. to 3:45 p.m. daily during November to March and run every 60 minutes; or from 9:45 a.m. to 5:15 p.m. daily during April to October and run every 45 minutes. Take a cultural journey through the most wonderful works of art in the city. Sights included on this route include:

- Piazza Municipo
- Piazza del Gesu
- Piazza Dante
- Museo Archeologico
- Museo di Capodimonte
- Catacombe S. Gennaro
- Bellini
- Porta Capuana
- Piazza Bovio/Universita

(2) **Line B - Naples Bay** (12 stops) - Runs from 10:15 a.m. to 4:15 p.m. daily during November to March, and runs every 60 minutes; or from 9:30 a.m. to 5:45 p.m. daily during April to October, and runs every 45 minutes. You get a beautiful view of Mount Vesuvius towering over the blue waters of the gulf on this tour as you travel along the majestic Villa Communale gardens past Mergellina, the Neapolitan's favorite sea promenade, and pass the fishing boats and ferries for the islands before slowly climbing the hillside towards Posillipo. Sights included on this route include:

- Piazza Municipo
- Santa Lucia
- Piazza Vittoria
- Villa Pignatelli
- Mergellina
- Posillipo
- Capo Posillipo
- Parco Virgiliano
- Via Petrarca
- Via Caracciolo/Mergellina
- Castel dell'Ovo/Via Parthenope
- Via Acton/Porto

(3) **Line C - San Martino** (9 stops) - Runs from 11:00 a.m. to 3:00 p.m. only on Saturdays and Sundays and takes 120 minutes to ride the full loop.

- Largo Castello (Piazza Municipo)
- Via Santa Lucia
- Piazza die Martiri
- PAN
- Piazza Amedeo
- Piazza Vanvitelli
- Largo San Martino
- Via Salvator Rosa
- Piazza Dante

WALKING TOUR OF NAPLES

If you PREFER A WALKING TOUR: To get your bearings as you begin your walk around the city, it is helpful to know that Naples is surrounded by the bay to the south and by low mountains all around. **Spaccanapoli**, which translates loosely as "divide Naples in half" and refers to the narrow, straight street that runs down its middle east-west like a Main Street and is laid out as a grid of narrow streets.

Sights To See in the City Center

A walking tour of Naples should include stops at the Duomo, or Cathedral of Naples, to visit its Treasure Chapel and Basilica Santa Restituta, the oldest church in Naples dating back to the 4th century, Plebiscite Square to see the Royal Palace, the beautiful church of St Francesco di Paula, the Town Hall Square and the New Castle built by the French Family of Anjou. Below are directions to these sights.

Since you are at the port, begin at t**he Waterfront District** which is just south of downtown Naples.

Via Toledo spills into Piazza Plebescito**,** the heart of 18th century Naples, with the Palazzo Reale [royal palace] and world-famous Teatro San Carlo, one of the oldest, largest, and most respected opera houses in Italy.

Beyond this is the long, wide harborside park of Chiaira**,** with a few blocks of buildings climbing up a small ridge. At the end of Chiaira to the north of the city center is a vast park, the city's major art museum and painting gallery, Museo Capodimonte, and the Catacombs of San Gennaro. Santa Chiara Church and Monastery built in Provencal Gothic style was the largest Clarissan church ever built. In the 17th to 18th centuries it was remodeled in Baroque style but after being almost destroyed during World War II, it was restored in what is believed to be its original form. The church holds the tombs of several kings and queens as well as relics of Saint Louis of Toulouse, including his brain.

From Santa Chiara, take *Via Benedetto* Croce to Piazza San Domenico Maggiore. On this square you'll see an obelisk built by the monks of San Martino after the plague of 1656 in which many people of Naples died (the monks saved themselves by shutting themselves inside the monastery). As you face the square, the building on the left is Palazzo Petrucci, the oldest building with its original entry and courtyard. Farther back is the entrance to the church of San Domenico Maggiore.

From Piazza San Domenico Maggiore, walk along *Via San Biago*. This street is **known as Spaccanapoli** because it splits the old center of Naples in half. The original Greek city of Neapolis was here and the area still retains the same narrow streets from Greek times. Spaccanapoli was one of the three main east-west Greek streets.

Stop in the Church of Sant'Angelo a Nilo to see the bas relief on the tomb of the tomb of Cardinal Brancacci by Donatello and Michelozzo and paintings by Marco Pino. Near the church in the small square, Piazzetta del Nilo, you'll see a large marble Roman statue dedicated to the Nile River.

Via San Gregorio Armeno is known as the street of Nativity workshops because it's lined with artisan workshops that make statuettes and scenery for the famous Neopalitan nativity scenes or presepi. Small storefronts selling nativity pieces and tourist items spill out onto the street while the best pieces are kept inside the tiny shops. About halfway up the street is the Church of San Gregorio Armeno. If you're there on a Tuesday morning, stop in to see the miracle of the liquefying blood being performed. At the end of *Via San Gregorio Armeno*, near the corner of *Via Tribunali* is the Church of San Lorenzo Maggiore. Excavations under the church reveal parts of the Roman city, including what was the Roman Forum.

On *Via Tribunali* there's an entrance to Naples Underground, a tour that takes you through the ancient aqueducts now buried under the modern city and there are also excavations under the Church of San Paolo Maggiore.

The Duomo, or Cathedral of Naples, is on *Via Duomo*. From *Via San Gregorio Armeno*, turn right on *Via dei Tribunali* and then left on *Via Duomo*. The Duomo is a 13th century Gothic cathedral dedicated to San Gennaro, Naple's patron saint. On one side of it is the 4th century Basilica Santa Restituta, the oldest church in Naples, with stunning ceiling frescoes and columns believed to be from the Temple of Apollo.

TIP #2: Beware of <u>pickpockets</u> the whole way – especially at the bus stop, on any bus/tram, and most especially on Piazza Garibaldi and in the train station.

TIP #3: Get a Taste of Local Flavor: <u>Pizza was invented in Naples</u>. Spigola (sea bass) is the most popular fish, and you'll find it served steamed and baked. For dessert, try sfogliatella, a delicious clam-shaped Neapolitan pastry.

<u>DAY TRIPS AWAY FROM NAPLES BY TRAIN AND FERRY</u>

<u>By Train:</u>

The lower level of the **Naples Central Train Station** houses the **Circumvesuviana**, the train that will take you to Mount Vesuvius, Pompeii, and Sorrento. **Walk the short distance from the cruise ship dock** to the suburban train line, **the *Ferrovia Circumvesuviana*** located **DOWNSTAIRS**. Address: Piazza Garibaldi. **Pompeii's** Scavi Station is just 35 minutes and Sorrento is about 55 to 68 minutes from Naples; and has trains running frequently throughout the day.

TIP #4: The train runs frequently **but not late at night**.

You can buy tickets for the Circumvesuviana from a ticket booth or an automated machine, and a simple one-way ticket will cost you less than €4. If you're making a day-trip of it and will be returning to Naples later on the same day, ask at the ticket booth about buying a ticket that's basically a day-long pass which will allow you to return to Naples anytime before midnight.

In Sorrento, you can board a **ferry** or **hydrofoil** for a beautiful trip across the Bay of Naples to the Isle of Capri.

DAY TRIP PLAN: SAVE THE AFTERNOON FOR CAPRI ISLAND–BEACH, CAVE & SHOPPING

Typical Cruise Ship Excursion:

*Mt. Vesuvius & Pompeii Hike - Hike to the summit of Mt. Vesuvius for incredible views of the volcano's crater and the Bay of Naples. Then take a guided walking tour of Pompeii; one of the world's most amazing archaeological wonders. HIGHLIGHTS: Hike the final 1,000 feet to the top of Mt. Vesuvius and enjoy the wonderful view from the rim. Explore Pompeii and see what Roman life was like in the 1st century AD. **Duration: 6 hours Prices starting from: $109.00 USD***

There are day trips you can take using the train and ferry line without spending $109.00 per person, and I would suggest the following trips for you if you'd like to enjoy everything Naples port has to offer. **I suggest you go to Capri Island in the afternoon** because most of the cruise excursions go to Capri in the morning and it is CROWDED.

TRAIN STOPS:

(1)   Herculaneum & Mount Vesuvius - Get off the train at Erculano Scavi station where you can catch a *Compagnia Trasporti Vesuviani* bus outside the station, or follow the street in front of the station to the excavations, a ten minute walk. Herculaneum was a town that was destroyed along with Pompeii. Mount Vesuvius is the volcano that destroyed Pompeii and Herculaneum.   At Mt. Vesuvius, climb to the summit of Vesuvius (takes approximately 45 minutes), and peer into the crater at 3,900 feet (1,200 meters) that caused the devastation that destroyed the city of Pompeii almost two thousand years ago; and see panoramic views of the beautiful Bay of Naples;

(2) Pompeii - Get off the train at Pompeii Scavi.   Pompeii was a thriving wealthy city that was buried by an eruption of Vesuvio in 79AD.   In Pompeii see the Forum, Thermal Baths, Vetti's House and Lupanare brothel, buried by volcanic ashes.   Pompeii reminds us of a tragedy, but at the same time, it is a living city, telling a story about itself, its inhabitants and life through objects, paintings and architecture.

(3) Castellammare di Stabia is a seaside town on the Bay of Naples with a castle and good seafood restaurants.

(4) Sorrento – last stop. Sorrento is a popular and quaint seaside resort on the Amalfi coast and is **the end of the train line**.

Sorrento is often thought of as part of the <u>Amalfi Coast</u>, but it's technically not. It's on what's known as the Sorrentine Peninsula across the Bay of Naples from the city of Naples. ****NOTE**: Sorrento is a town in two parts – the part that's near the water and the port, and the part that's overhead on top of the cliffs. The train arrives in the end of town of Sorrento, up on the cliffs. **To get to the water port requires a city bus ride or taxi**.

<u>**From Sorrento, take a ferry or hydrofoil to the Isle of Capri and then take another ferry back to Naples**</u>.

ISLE OF CAPRI

*"Il giorno del giudizio,
per gli Amalfitani che
andranno in paradiso
sará un giorno come
tutti gli altri."*

For the people of Amalfi
who go to heaven, judgment
day will be a day like any other.
—Renato Fucini

Ferries run from Sorento's main marina, **Marina Grande** [or to and **from Naple's marina,** Molo Beverello/Stazione Marittima] to the islands of Capri [approximately 45-50-minute cruise].

Travel to Capri is a highlight of a Naples vacation. Capri is an enchanting and picturesque island made of limestone rock. A favorite with Roman emperors, the rich and famous, artists, and writers, it's still one of the Mediterranean's must-see places. Lemon trees, flowers, and birds are abundant here, and beaches are also scattered around the island so you may want to sunbathe while visiting.

You will arrive by ferry boat [or hydrofoil] at *Marina Grande*. There are only two towns - *Capri*, just above Marina Grande, and *Anacapri*, the higher town. The funicular railway (*funiculare*) takes visitors up the hill from Marina Grande where your ferry arrives to the town of Capri. Or you can board a minibus for transfer to Anacapri. To get to Mount Solaro, the highest and most panoramic spot on the island, there's a chair lift from Anacapri during the day.

The island's top attractions: The Blue Grotto, *Grotta Azzurra*, is the most fascinating of the island's many sights. To enter the cave you take a small rowboat from near the cave entrance. Once inside, refraction of sunlight into the cave makes an iridescent blue light in the water. In addition, wander the island's quaint streets and explore its shops and cafés. Discover La_Piazzetta Square, which is surrounded by intriguing old buildings; the Gardens of Augustus that overlooks the famous Faraglioni, a famed offshore rock outcropping, and Marina Piccola. You can enjoy the spectacular views of the sea and sky from Anacapri. Take the funicular back down to Marina Grande, where you will board your ferry or hydrofoil for the return trip to Naples marina and walk, a bus, or taxi back to the cruise ship.

TIP #4: Be sure to sample **limoncello**, the local lemon liqueur, and the prized mozzarella di bufala [buffalo milk cheese].

Alternatively, you can take a hydrofoil from Naples to Sorrento or Capri and back to Naples

- **Alilauro Hydrofoil – The hydrofoil is the fastest option to travel around the coast of Naples.** Hydrofoils run regularly back and forth from Naples to Sorrento to Capri, but make sure you **check the schedule (it changes depending on the season) so that you don't miss the last one**. Hydrofoils are operated by Alilauro and depart from the pier called Moro Beverello in Naples near the Piazza Municipio. The trip will take about 40 minutes one-way and a one-way ticket will cost €11. Hydrofoils move so quickly that you won't be allowed to go outside during the trip. You can see the city and the mountain from the windows, but it's not ideal for picture-taking. It can also be a choppy ride, so if you're prone to seasickness you might want to choose a smoother-moving ferry.

CIVITAVECCHIA (ROME), ITALY

Typical Cruise Ship Excursion:

Imperial Rome - *Imperial Rome's fascinating history is revealed during your exploration of important sites. Maximize your time by avoiding ticket lines when entering the Roman Forum and Colosseum. HIGHLIGHTS: Visit Trevi Fountain and the Roman Forum. Step inside the Colosseum and discover St. Peter's Basilica. A local lunch is included in your journey through Imperial Rome. Headsets and a map of Rome are provided. NOTES: Travel time to and from Rome is about 1 1/2 hours each way.* **Approximate Duration: 10 hour(s) 30 minute(s) Prices starting from: $199.00 USD (Adult)**

Rome, the Eternal City, is the capital of modern Italy. **Save your money and explore the amazing history, culture, ancient monuments, interesting medieval churches, beautiful fountains, museums, and Renaissance palaces of Rome on your own for the purchase of a train ticket.** Before touring the city of Rome, experience the heart of the Roman Catholic religion with a visit to the Vatican City to explore St. Peter's Square, St. Peter's Basilica [the largest church in the world], the Sistine Chapel [a masterpiece of Renaissance art, the ceiling of which was painted by Michelangelo] and the Vatican Museum, that houses the largest art collection in the world. Once in Rome, begin at the Colosseum, Roman Forum, the Pantheon before proceeding to the famous Trevi Fountain where you can toss a coin into the fountain, to ensure that you'll always return to Rome.

Getting to the Train Station for Trip to Vatican City and Rome

TRENITALIA
GRUPPO FERROVIE DELLO STATO ITALIANE provides service from the Civitavecchia Train Station to St. Peters Basilica and to Rome.

There is a train station in the town of Civitavecchia [Cruise Ship Port] with several trains per hour going to Vatican City & Central Rome (Roma Termini). The train trip will take about 1 hour and 20 minutes, although there are some faster trains that can make it in under an hour.

The station is close to the entrance of the port but the port is quite a distance from where passengers usually disembark, therefore, Cruise passengers can catch a shuttle to the entrance of the port and walk 4 blocks to the train station. The train station is an easy 10-minute walk from the port entrance.

To find the trains station, simply exit the port entrance and then cross the street where the crosswalk is (you will see a newsstand on the other corner). Continue along this street (parallel to the coastline) for approximately 4 blocks until you hit the train station. It couldn't be easier. Once at the station, **purchase your round trip-ticket to Rome** and make your way out to the appropriate track that the train will stop at. ***The best ticket to buy is the B.I.R.G., as it will allow you to have unlimited train for 24 hours and also includes unlimited use of the underground [subway] in Rome, as well as the city buses.** The cost per person as of September, 2011 was about $50.00 round-trip. Be sure to validate your ticket in each of

the little yellow validation machines in the train terminals before you board.

You can go to St. Peters Square to visit Vatican City first and then get back on the train and go to Rome's Historic Center.

FIRST STOP = I would strongly suggest first going to St. Peters Square, (you will see St. Peters Dome before arriving at the station, so keep an eye out.)

Roma S. Pietro Make your way into the train station and leave through the front door. Turn left and continue down the hill until you hit the first street. Turn right one block and then continue to your left until you hit the main street (next block). Cross the street and continue along the street until the next left turn. You will see the columns making up St. Peters Square's fabulous borders. Simply enter St. Peters Square through the columns. Note that the entrance to St. Peters Basilica is on the right hand side as your look at the basilica. **NOTE: Ladies must not wear shorts or have their shoulders exposed,** as they will not be allowed to enter the basilica. **Men** will not be allowed into the basilica in **tank tops**. The same is true if you plan to visit the Vatican Museum. Inside the Vatican city you will find Vatican Museums, Michelangelo's Sistine Chapel, and the Vatican Gardens.

SECOND STOP = BOARD THE TRAIN & HEAD TO ROME - Suggested Itinerary – ***Get a Map***

ROMA TERMINI The sign for the Main Train Station in Rome is several stops after St. Peters. It arrives at **Tracks 27 - 30** in Rome's Main Train Station.

The best place to begin and end a walking tour of Rome's awesome sights is at the **Spanish Steps (Piazza di Spagna)**. From the Spanish Steps, you can easily take in, the Colosseum, the Pantheon, the Forum, Trevi Fountain and the Arch of Constantine, among other sights. Here's how:

<u>Upon arriving at Rome Termini</u>, to begin your tour of Rome you can either:

(1) Remain in the terminal and take the escalator down to the **Metro** - For 4 euros you can ride the Metro for up to six hours and stop and tour many of Rome's most famous sights. The 2 lines are the **red line is Metro A** (linea A) and the **blue is Metro B** (linea B). They cross at Rome's central station, Rome Termini. **They run from 5:30am to 11:30pm**;

(2) Walk out of the terminal and cross the street where you can board a **bus** [WARNING: Buses are used by locals and are VERY crowded];

Tickets for both the bus system and Metro can be purchased from a tabacchi (tobacco shop), a bar, or vending machines at metro stations and major bus stops. A single ticket costs €1 and is good for a single metro ride or 75 minutes on the busses. A daily ticket (B.I.G.) is available for €4.

(3) Walk out of the terminal and begin your **walking tour of Rome – This is truly the most convenient way to see Rome** – you will walk for hours but you will follow a path with all of the other walkers and you won't miss a single sight. **Along the path, you will encounter a cobblestone area with shops and restaurants as well as a contemporary shopping district**.

WALKING [OR METRO] TOUR OF ROME

Walk out of the train terminal and ask anyone what direction to begin walking to the Colosseum – anyone can point you in the right direction and from there it is a piece of cake to follow the paths to see all of Rome. Pick up a map [like the one shown in this chapter] outside the station.

1. **First stop** - the *Colosseo* (**Colosseum**) [Metro is the Colosseo stop]. When you arrive, you will first see Capitoline Hill located between the Forum and the Campus Martius. Capitoline Hill is one of the seven famous hills of Rome. It was the citadel of the earliest Romans and contains several ancient ground-level ruins and Medieval and Renaissance palaces and the Victor Emanuel Monument . This significant urban plan was designed by Michelangelo. Be prepared to marvel at the architecture of this magnificent arena. The line of tourists may look forbidding but even if you don't have a reservation, I found out that **you can skip the lines altogether by going to the *Guided Audio Tour* ticket window and for 15 euros get a ticket into the Colosseum**. You can also just walk around the outskirts of the Colosseum.

2. **From the *Colosseo*, follow the other tourists on a walkway towards the *Foro Romano*** (Roman Forum), the old heart of the Roman Empire. As you walk down into the Forum along a masonry ramp, you'll be heading for Via Sacra, the ancient Roman road that ran through the Forum connecting the Capitoline Hill, to your right, with the Arch of Titus (1st c. A.D.), off

to your left. You will stroll by temple ruins, basilicas and museums on Capitol Hill.

3. **The Palatine Hill -** Next head up the Clivus Palatinus -- the road to the palaces of the Palatine Hill, or *Palatino.* With your back to the Arch of Titus, it's the road going up the hill to the left. It was on the Palatine Hill that Rome first became a city. Legend tells us that the date was 753 B.C. The new city originally consisted of nothing more than the Palatine, which was soon enclosed by a surprisingly sophisticated wall, remains of which can still be seen on the Circus Maximus side of the hill.

4. **Next, follow the tourists and head towards the** *Fontana Di Trevi*, the **Trevi Fountain**. On your walk, you will pass Palatine Hill, Circus Maximus, and the Thermal Baths of Caracalla and then pass through the narrow twisting cobblestone streets to the Trevi Fountain. Trevi Fountain is crowded with countless tourists but it is a visual feast for the eyes. The Baroque fountain of Neptune is a famous gathering spot and an excellent area to grab *gelato,* Italian ice cream.

4. The **Pantheon** is a brief 5-10 minute walk from the Trevi Fountain and offers another glimpse of the splendor of Rome.

5. **Last** you will head to the Spanish Steps at *Piazza Di Spagna*, another famous meeting spot for tourists, for your return to the cruise ship. The Metro is located nearby and quickly transports you back to Rome Termini for your return trip home.

Sights to See On Your Walk:

All of the Sights to See in Rome – you can add any of these additional sights to the tour above **[they are included in your map of Rome – like the one below].**

- Baths of Caracalla
- Bioparco (zoo)
- Campidoglio
- Castel Sant'Angelo
- Circus Maximus
- The Colosseum
- Imperial Forums
- The Mamertine Prison
- Ostia Antica
- The Pantheon
- Piazza del Popolo
- Piazza Navona
- Protestant Cemetery
- The Spanish Steps
- Trevi Fountain
- Via Appia Antica
- Villa Borghese Gardens
- Pincio Gardens

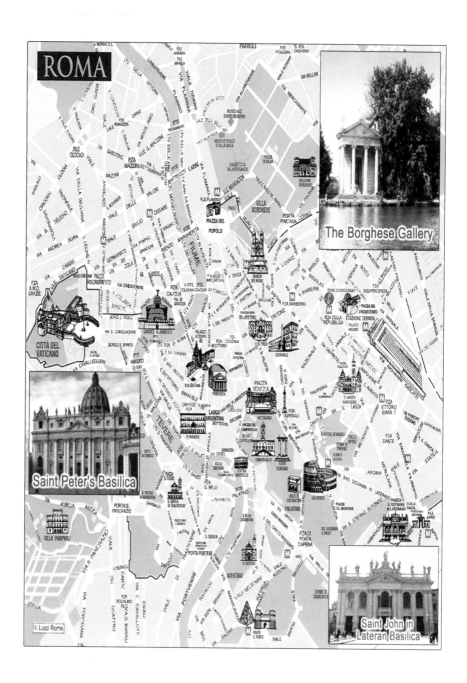

ROMA

The Borghese Gallery

Saint Peter's Basilica

Saint John in Lateran Basilica

44

Returning to Cruise Ship Port from Rome

Be aware that the tracks for the Civitavecchia train operate on (27-30) are quite a distance from the rest of the station and take about 10 minutes to reach on foot.

When you get off of the train at the port area, you need to catch the shuttle, which leaves and drops off passengers from the ships at the Michelangelo Fortress - you can't miss it - a large stone fortress inside the port area. From there, the bus swings through the dock area and the shuttle leaves people at whichever ship they are taking. There's a lack of taxis. So it's best not to count on getting a taxi.

TIP #5: *Get a Taste of Local Flavor of Rome - There are many varieties of pasta available with a wide range of sauces. Bucatini all'Amatricana, a thick spaghetti in a tangy tomato and bacon sauce, is one example associated with Rome. Osso Bucco, also popular, is a casserole of veal shin flavored with garlic, tomatoes and wine. For dessert, try ricotta cake, a form of cheesecake, or Zuppa Inglese, a liqueur-soaked sponge cake covered with custard, similar to English trifle.*

LIVORNO (PISA/FLORENCE), ITALY

Pisa and Florence are most noted as the birthplace of the Renaissance. Highlights include impressive piazzas and some of the finest examples of Florentine Gothic architecture and design from the 15th Century. You will take a shuttle bus ride from the cruise ship port to the center of Livorna and then board a train to Pisa and Florence.

While in Livorna, (1) take a short boat tour to see the canals of Livorna, and then (2) board the train to Pisa and Florence. Or (3) you can skip the following description of the boat tour of Livorna and go directly to the train station in Livorna and go to Pisa and Florence.

Tour of Livorna

Typical Cruise Ship Excursion:

Livorno Boat Tour - *This tour delivers the highlights and history of Livorno on a boat ride to through its channels. You'll also enjoy free time at the Old Market to shop or explore at your own pace. HIGHLIGHTS: Board a motorboat for a cruise along the Livorno channels that cover centuries of Livorno's history and cruise through New Venice. Enjoy a guided walk of Republic Square and Old Market. You'll also have free time at the Old Market to shop or explore at your own pace.* **Duration: 2 hours Prices starting from: $39.00 USD**

Getting from the Port of Livorno to Livorna City Centre:

Your cruise ship docks at at the industrial wharfs in Livorno Port. There is **shuttle bus** service into town which drops you off and picks you up in Piazza del Municipio, opposite **Livorno Town Hall** (Comune), just behind Piazza Grande. **The charge is €5 per person round trip**.

One of the best and most relaxing ways to see Livorno and is to take a boat trip along the canals, or *fossi*. The tour offers an interesting perspective of the city and takes you around the Fosso Reale (Royal Canal), past the Fortezza Nuova (New Fortress) and right under the Piazza della Repubblica. **Tickets cost €10-12**

euros and are available from the Tourist Information office in Via Pieroni. **Trips are offered at 12.30pm, 2.30pm and 3.30pm.**

Getting to the Train Station for Trip to Pisa and Florence

Take the **shuttle bus** from the port to Piazza del Municipio in the center of Livorna and walk across street to Piazza Grande. Buy a Bus Ticket [**cost €1.20**] at one of the **news kiosks** in Piazza del Municipio or Piazza Grande. **Take the No. 1 or No. 2 Bus from Piazza Grande to Livorno Centrale Train Station**. [Be sure to stamp your ticket in one of the **blue machines** when you board the bus.]

Livorna Train Station

The trains to Pisa and Florence run every hour and the train trip from Livorno to Pisa takes 15-20 minutes and the train trip from Livorno to Florence takes about 1 hour and thirty minutes. The train fare to and from Livorno Florence is around **€16.40 per person**.

Make sure you **stamp your tickets BEFORE** you get on the train. Small validating machines on the walls are all over the station.

Walking Tour of Pisa

Typical Cruise Ship Excursion:

> ***Pisa On Your Own*** *–You'll pass just outside of the port town of Livorno for a 30-minute **drive** to the once-powerful city of Pisa. Upon arrival, a short walk will take you to the Field of Miracles, where you will see one of the world's most amazing sights the Campanile, or Leaning Tower. Your tour escort will give you free time to explore on your own each of the magnificent buildings in the Piazza. During your free time, you can shop or take photos. Participants are provided with a Pisa map.* ***Approximate Duration: 3 hours Prices starting from: $42.00 USD***

So you can spend $42.00 per person to go on a 3-hour excursion to see Pisa on your own! Put your wallet away and follow the plan below to see Pisa on your own in about an hour! It is quick and easy to get from **Livorno Centrale station to Pisa** by train. The journey to Pisa only takes 15-20 minutes for only €2.30 each way per person.

When you **arrive in Pisa by train**, it is still about 1.5km from the station to the **Leaning Tower** in Piazza dei Miracoli. You can either **walk or take the local bus**.

Walking from Pisa Centrale Station to the Leaning Tower at Piazza dei Miracoli

The **most direct route** is to head away from the station towards the big **Piazza Vittorio Emanuele**. Turn left here into **Via Nino Bixio**, and then right into **Via Francesco Crispi**. Follow this road to the river, go over the **Arno River** on the Solferino **bridge**, and then go straight down **Via Roma** which brings you directly to **Piazza dei Miracoli** and the Tower of Pisa!

Gateway to Piazza dei Miracoli   **Piazza dei Miracoli**

 A longer but more interesting route is to take *Corso Italia* from Piazza Vittorio Emanuele. This <u>shopping street</u> leads to the Arno River where you cross on the *Ponte di Mezzo*. Then follow **Borgo Stretto** which leads straight ahead from the bridge. Turn left into **Via Dini** and follow this to **Piazza dei Cavalieri**. Go through the square and head past the little church of San Rocco, down **Via dei Mille** and then right into **Via Santa Maria** which leads to the **Leaning Tower of Pisa**.

<u>Bus from Pisa Centrale Statin to the Leaning Tower at Piazza dei Miracoli</u>

 Before you leave **Pisa Centrale train station**, go to the news kiosk in the station foyer and **buy a bus ticket** for the journey to and from the **Leaning Tower**. The bus ticket costs about €1.10 each way.

The **bus stop** to the **Leaning Tower** is directly across the street from the station, right in front of the **Pisa Jolly Hotel**. The orange bus you need is a **LAM Rossa** (**RED**) bus. This bus takes about 10 minutes and will take you to the **Torre** bus stop which is very close to the **Tower of Pisa**. For the return trip from the Tower to the train station you can catch the same bus from the other side of the road.

If you have time and would like to do a little walking after visiting the Leaning Tower, you can walk to the **Arno River** and instead of returning to the Tower, you can pick up the same **Lam Rossa** bus just before it crosses over the **Ponte di Mezzo**.

NOW BACK TO THE TRAIN AND HEAD TO FLORENCE

Typical Cruise Ship Excursion:

> *Florence On Your Own* - *Go off on your own in this Renaissance city, armed with insider tips from your Tour Director. Explore this glorious city at your leisure. HIGHLIGHTS: After a 1 ½ hour transfer, your escort will designate a meeting time and place and then you will have approximately 6 hours to see the sights, shop or enjoy a meal at your leisure and pace. This tour does not include lunch or entrance fees.* ***Approximate Duration: 9 hours 30 minutes Prices starting from: $89.00 USD***

So you can spend $89.00 per person to go on a cruise line excursion to see Florence on your own! Put your wallet away and follow the plan below to see Florence on your own! Livorno Port, in the Tuscan region of Italy, is ideally located for exploring Florence and Pisa, two of the most beautiful cities in Italy.

Florence Walking Tour

The Florence Train Station (**Firenze Santa Maria Novella Station**) is located near central Florence and is a walkable distance away from major attractions in Florence. **Keep in mind** that the most famous sights of Florence are at Piazza della Signoria across the Arno River on the Ponte Vecchio. If you are short on time, skip Steps 1-4 below and go straight to the most famous square, Piazza della Signoria, to see the Statue of David and other Renaissance works. *Galleria degli Uffizi* holds the world's most important collection of Renaissance art but it's also Italy's most crowded museum [Be sure to buy tickets ahead to avoid long lines].

WALKING TOUR OF FLORENCE [See List of IMPORTANT PLACES TO SEE below]

1. Start in Piazza San Marco. From the train station, walk on *Via Navionale* to Piazza Independenza, then turn right on *Via Ventisette Aprile* and see the Florence Baptistry, which is an octagonal shaped religious building that across from the Duomo [or cathedral] and the Giotto [or bell tower], which are examples of Romanesque-Gothic style architecture.

Piazza San Marco and San Marco Museum   Duomo, or cathedral, and Baptistery

From the Duomo and Baptistery, walk on *Via Martelli* and continue straight on *Via Cavour*.

2. Cross Piazza San Marco to the San Marco church and museum - inside the church you will see the altar crucifix by Fra Angelico. Upstairs you will see the *Annunciation*, one of Fra Angelico's most famous works. Then go into the interesting *Museo di San Marco* beside the church to see the monk's cells with painted frescoes by Fra Beato Angelico, relics of Savonarola, and artifacts from medieval Florence. You can also see the cell and

51

relics of another famous resident, Savonarola, who was the righteous monk who decried the decadence of Florence's art to end the Renaissance period.

3. Next go to the Piazza dell Mercato Centrale [or central market]: Exit the museum and turn right and walk past the *Galleria dell' Accademia*, then turn right on *Via degli Alfani* and left on *Via Sant Orsola*. The central market was once the main shopping center in Florence for fresh foods, like cow stomachs and intestines, sold in outside stalls. Now the market is of interest to the tourist because many of the shops sell local Tuscan products [wine, biscotti, cheeses, salami] as well as, leather goods, clothing, and souvenirs. *You can* try out a *lampredotto*, a cow's stomach sandwich, at the Nerbonne Restaurant which has been around since 1872 and is very popular with locals.

4. Walk on the street that continues along the river until you get to the Ponte Vecchio, or old bridge, lined with shops. Ponte Vecchio, built in 1345, was the first bridge in Florence to cross the Arno River. It is also the only medieval bridge to survive the bombings of World War II. Ponte Vecchio became a top place for gold and silver shopping in Renaissance Florence, and it is still lined with shops selling gold and leather products.

Across the Arno River is another good area for lunch is. One of favorite restaurants is *Trattoria Sabatino*, just across the bridge on Ponte Vespucci. As you continue walking in this area, you will find several stores with homemade gelato in a variety of flavors that you must try even if you are full from lunch!

5.   **Continue touring the most famous sights of Florence** while aross the river on the Ponte Vecchio. Continue walking straight to the most famous square, Piazza della Signoria (slightly off to the right) to see the heart of the historic center and a free open-air sculpture exhibit. The *Loggia della Signoria* holds some <u>important statues</u> including a **copy of Michelangelo's David**. *Galleria dell' Academia* holds **Michelangelo's David, the most famous sculpture in the world**, as well as other sculptures by Michelangelo and a collection of musical instruments. *Galleria degli Uffizi* holds the **world's** <u>**most important collection of Renaissance art**</u> but it's also <u>**Italy's most crowded museum [Be sure to buy tickets ahead to avoid long lines]**</u>; and *Palazzo Vecchio*, with its elaborately decorated public rooms and private apartments also sits on the piazza.

6. Next exit the Piazza della Signoria **on the north and walk up Via dei Cerchi** to Florence's oldest building, a tower from the ninth century, *Torre Bizantina della Pagliuzza*. Cross Via del Corso and continue straight on Via Sant Elisabetta, then look for the *Hotel Brunelleschi* on the left. **Inside the tower part of the hotel is a private museum with medieval ceramics found during the restoration and the remains of a Roman bath (one of the few Roman remains in Florence**).

Torre Bizantina della Pagliuzza

7. **Now back track to *Via del Corso*** and turn right to get to the next piazza, Piazza della Repubblica. As you enter the piazza, you'll see a big arch with an inscription on top that refers to this area of Florence as squalor that had to be cleaned up and given new life. What was once an important market center in medieval times became the modern Piazza della Repubblica

when Florence was the capital of the newly unified country of Italy (1865-1871). Giubbe Rosse is a farmous eatery in the square that is filled with contemporary art.

Piazza della Repubblica

9. **Your walking tour ends here**. You will **make your way back to the train station** by walking back across the Ponte Vecchio, or old bridge. To return to Piazza San Marco, exit the square the way you came in. Turn left on Via dei Calzaiuoli, pass through Piazza San Givoanni and continue straight. This becomes Via Cavour and leads to Piazza San Marco. Follow steps in Step 1 backwards to return to the train station if you haven't seen a short-cut on the way. [Turn Left on *Via Ventisette Aprile* and walk on *Via Navionale* to Piazza Independenza.]

TIP #6: Piazza San Marco is a major bus hub so it's pretty easy to get there by bus from anywhere in Florence. The number 7 bus from Fiesole stops in Piazza San Marco.

IMPORTANT PLACES TO SEE ALONG YOUR WALKING TOUR:

Il Duomo - Cathedral of Santa Maria del Fiore - most popular site is the huge 1296 Gothic Duomo the *Cathedral de Santa Maria del Fiore.* Its exterior of green, pink, & white marble has elaborate doors and interesting statues. Inside, Brunelleschi's Dome is a masterpiece of construction. **Buy a ticket to climb the 463 steps to its top**.

The Baptistery - John the Baptist, is one of Florence's oldest buildings, with exterior of green & white marble and 3 sets of bronze doors. Inside, see mosaics and a marble pavement of the zodiac.

Campinile - Bell Tower - The first story was designed by Giotto and it is commonly called *Giotto's Campinile*. Buy a ticket and climb the 414 stairs (no lift) for great views of the Cathedral and its dome and the city of Florence and surroundings.

Boboli Garden and Pitti Palace - a huge park on a hillside behind the Pitti Palace. Visit **8 different galleries, including art, costumes, jewelry, and apartments**.

Santa Croce - largest Franciscan church - holds the tombs of several important Florentines including Michelangelo and Dante. Interior contains exceptional stained glass windows and frescoes. Brunelleschi's most important work, the *Cappella dei Pazzi*, is in *Santa Croce*.

Shopping - The most famous shopping is around *Piazza San Lorenzo*. Another good place is *Mercato Nuovo (Porcellino)* on *Via Porta Rossa*. *Mercato Centrale is* great for food shopping.

Tip #7: RETURN TO LIVORNA FROM FLORENCE: Trains from Florence to Livorno depart every hour at 27 minutes past the hour. The train that leaves at 3:27 arrives in Livorno 4:49) and is probably **the latest train you can catch in order to reboard a cruise ship before it leaves Port**. Most ships in Livorno Port leave around 6pm

Tip #8: On the way back you could **save time by getting a taxi** from Livorno Centrale station directly to the ship (make a note of the dock name - probably **Varco Valessini** or **Varco Galvani**, but there are a couple of new ones too).

DON'T FORGET TO VALIDATE YOUR TRAIN TICKET AT ONE OF THE MACHINES IN THE STATION BEFORE YOU TRAVEL. There is a fine of 100 Euros if you are found travelling without a validated ticket. Validate before each journey.

Made in the USA
Lexington, KY
23 March 2016